WADE SCHUMAN

Aspects of View

DECEMBER 13, 2001 - JANUARY 26, 2002

Forum Gallery

745 FIFTH AVENUE AT 57TH STREET, NEW YORK

WADE SCHUMAN

AT FIRST Wade Schuman's West 38th Street studio seems classic New York—a reconstructed sweat shop with exposed pipes and, something every history minded painter ought to have, a view of the Hudson. He's also got an esoteric collection of taxidermy, including a pangolin, two cassowaries, a rumpless bantam and a toad; and some interesting bones, including a bison mandible and some whale vertebrae. Parts of his collection came from his great-grandfather Henry Turner Bailey, the painter, architect, writer, art educator and bird watcher from Massachusetts. And some have more to do with his daily life (a stack of vintage amplifiers and an armory of rare harmonicas tie in to his role as leader of the band, Hazmat Modine.) Bundles of *Komar and Melamid's RBS Gazette* fill one corner—he's the magazine's Creative Director; and leaning up against one wall are stacks and stacks of easels—evidence of his teaching. The piles of stuff look like still-lives begging to be painted, and it's easy to forget you're just around the corner from Times Square.

"One of the great deals about being an artist is that you can spend hours just looking at things," Schuman says. "At their beauty and complexity and oddness. It's a privilege to be able to do that and to do that is to appreciate fundamental aspects of reality." That said, his observational skills and technical mastery are tools at the service of his ideas. He's not after realism, but alternative realities, constructed by manipulating objects', size, space, and proportion, in unnerving, non-literal color.

To begin to explain what his work is, Schuman describes an experience he had when he was sixteen. While hiking the Appalachian Trail he came across a deer carcass partially submerged in a stream and covered with pulsating monarch butterflies. He was struck by the juxtaposition of beauty and death, of delicate, refined creatures tangled with a metaphor for the finality of the physical world. "There's something intrinsically ironic about creating an image," says Schuman, "Because what you make is constant but the thing you observed decays. That object speaks to you about what it means to be a living creature."

"Aspects of View" is organized around three related bodies of work—with points of view shifting from macro to micro—from the exterior world to the interior world to the world of small objects. The paintings are circular, ovoid or arched. Schuman says he never found a good reason for the rectangles artists take as a given, with their disingenuous suggestion of objectivity. Like altarpiece panels or heraldic devices, Schuman's shapes imply selectivity, metaphor, meaning. The shape around *Embrace*— the man and woman locked in an ambiguous clinch— turns the image into an emblem of the duality and struggle inherent in intimacy.

Passages, a triptych completed over five years, is a somewhat autobiographical account of growth. The left predella depicts the street in Ann Arbor, Michigan, where the artist grew up. It's a tranquil summer night in suburbia and the landscape has become an extension of life indoors—gorgeous puddles of light break the neighborhood up into warm rooms with interior dramas spilling right out from nearby homes. The right predella is a reversed mirror image: a street scene with lights going off into the distance on a cold winter day in the city. It's Schuman's street, West 38th, in one of those snowstorms that shuts down the city—showing that the most urban environment can still be taken over by nature. The central panel shows a journey in a small rowboat. The view from above lends a womb-like aspect to the boat which, like the coffee cup balanced on the seat, is a precarious vessel for such a dangerous passage--the handling of the dark water alone describes the profundity of the voyage.

Historical consciousness underlies Schuman's work. *Then and Now* is, in one sense, a contemporary Vanitas painting (death is symbolized by a fly, sweetness by the overripe flesh of a melon, bitterness and wasted energy by spilt coffee). In the same image, Schuman pays Vermeer-like attention to the window's light and makes iconographic reference to Van Eyck's *Arnofini Wedding Portrait.* It has its own deep resonance: the woman with the bird in the painting on the wall is the same as the one who appears in the room with the cock in the foreground, sixteen years later. Hints that things are out of balance suggest a turning point in a complicated relationship.

Schuman's first love was Zoology, and animals still dominate his work. Their symbolic power is heightened by their appearance at moments of transitional consciousness, with figures who often seem to be coming in or out of sleep. The man at the center of *Conversation,* perhaps Schuman's most intriguing and disturbing painting, appears lost in dissolute thought as he's advised by a blandly wraithlike figure, and presides over the shambles of a feast circled by a pack of dogs. "Dogs are one of the few animals that still have currency as a metaphor," says Schuman. "We've made them the most like us. Angry. Crazy. Jealous. They mirror our emotional states."

In *Woman with Pig* the elegant opposing curves of the havalina's spine and the nude's torso suggest an uneasy aftermath. "If you didn't grow up with animals, they probably seem quite alien," Schuman says. "But we're much closer to a pig than the things we think we feel close to—a tree, or a building." It's the kind of juxtaposition that drives much of his work, the kind that can unearth metaphor and narrative out of the mundane. Housecats create a feeling of anxiousness in the six foot diameter circular painting, *Man Entering Room (Reoccurrence).* It's also a good example of Schuman's approach to narrative: though the bonsai tree suggests the passage of many years, the image is not stuck on one point of time, or one particular story line.

In his small paintings, *Observations,* we find an exploration of the still-life tradition severed from traditional iconography and traditional perspective: these all look downward. *Crab in a Pan* is especially arresting because it's an iconic image—a bluefin crab stuck in a skillet whose thorny armor and beautiful Technicolored claws are useless against this dumb cast iron threat. This embodiment of defensiveness, ironically trapped, is elevated to metaphoric status by the intensity of the painting, the clarity of the observation. Schuman calls *Fish with Bones,* a painting about the "drama of the interrelatedness of existence. Sometimes you're walking in the woods, you look down and you see a subsection of the universe." The fish seems dumbfounded at its predicament, resting in the woods. *Hand with Bee* instills a sense of vertigo, and more peculiarly the sensation of noticing something out of the corner of the eye. "Sometimes," says Schuman, "it's that accidentally poetic, brief moment of drama that is so revelatory about the world."

Wade Schuman is not content to churn out the high concept one liners that so many artists build their careers on. Not content to rely on the easy beauty of technical perfection, of lifelike drapery and seductive flesh, he's a conceptualist. His complex paintings are commentaries on existence, elaborate constructions—they are the pictorial equivalent of installation art—with a rigorous intellectual edge. A conversation with Schuman is an urgent chase—as he paces and waves his coffee cup—from historical reference to aesthetic thought to philosophical point. What he admired most about his turn of the century great grandfather was his tremendous energy and positive belief in his ability to pursue his disparate interests. Schuman's genius is in doggedly following wherever his investigations lead him. While he agrees that art should boil things down to the essential, he says, "The essential isn't simple, it's complex. And I like that complexity." The rich visual imagery in his work is constantly transforming to keep up with the challenge inherent in his thinking. His remarkable work, the manifestation of his unique view, is deeply resonant with the contemporary world and an exciting development in painting.

—OWEN PHILLIPS

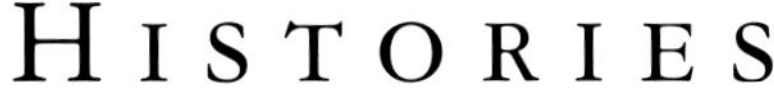# Histories

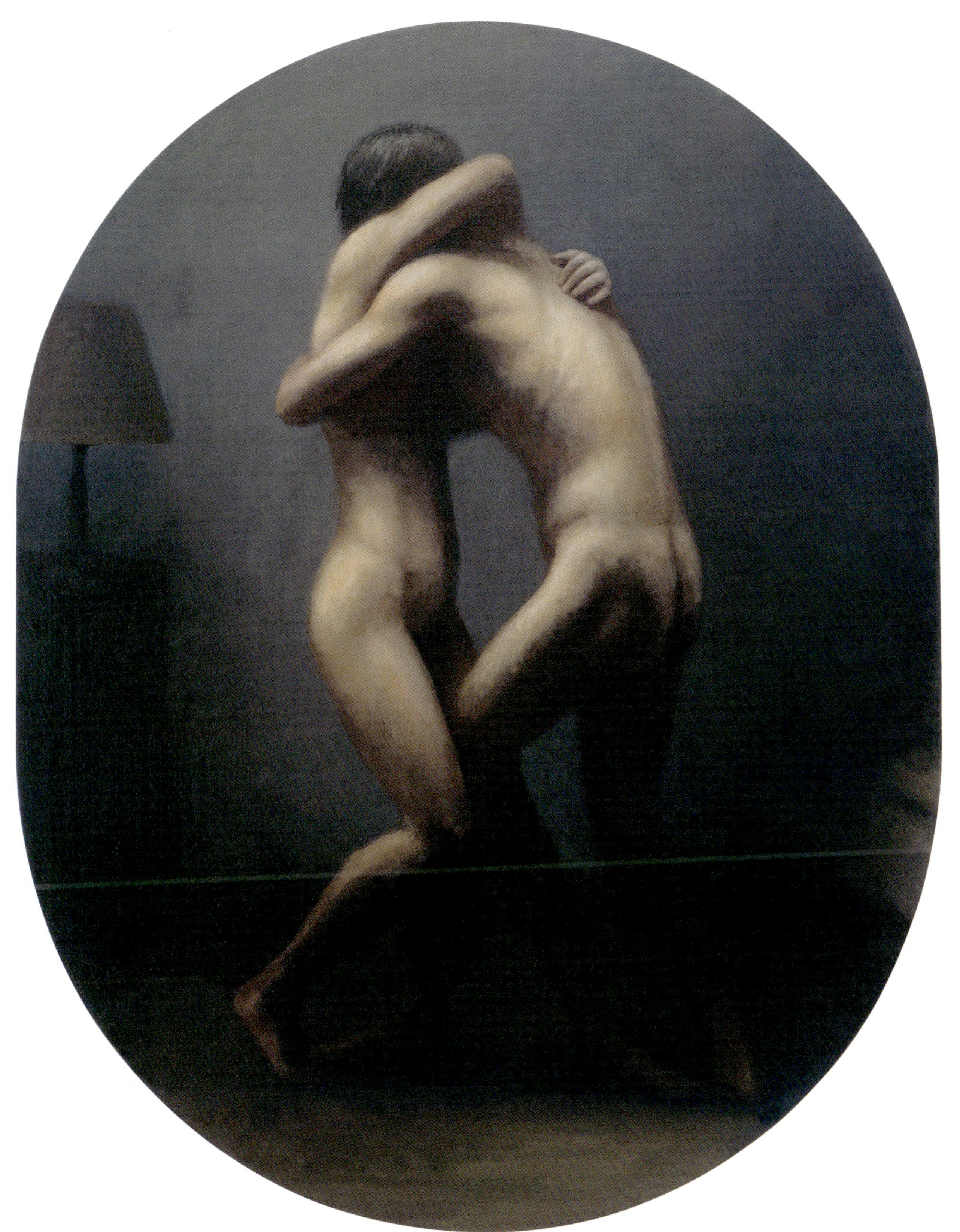

Passages (conflict)

1996

Oil on linen

37.5 x 35.5 inches

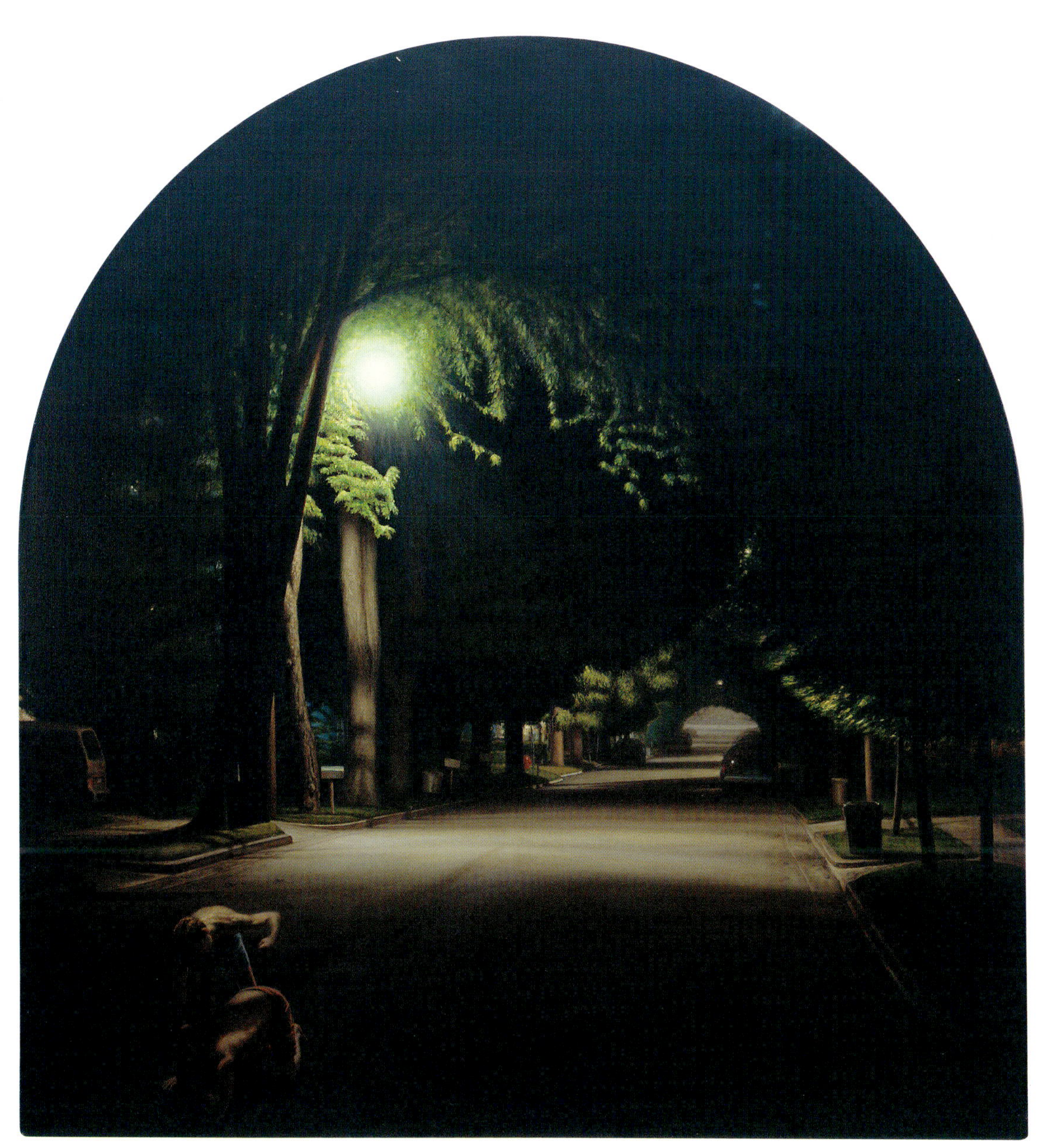

Passages (rowing man)

1998–1999

Oil on linen

66 x 48 inches

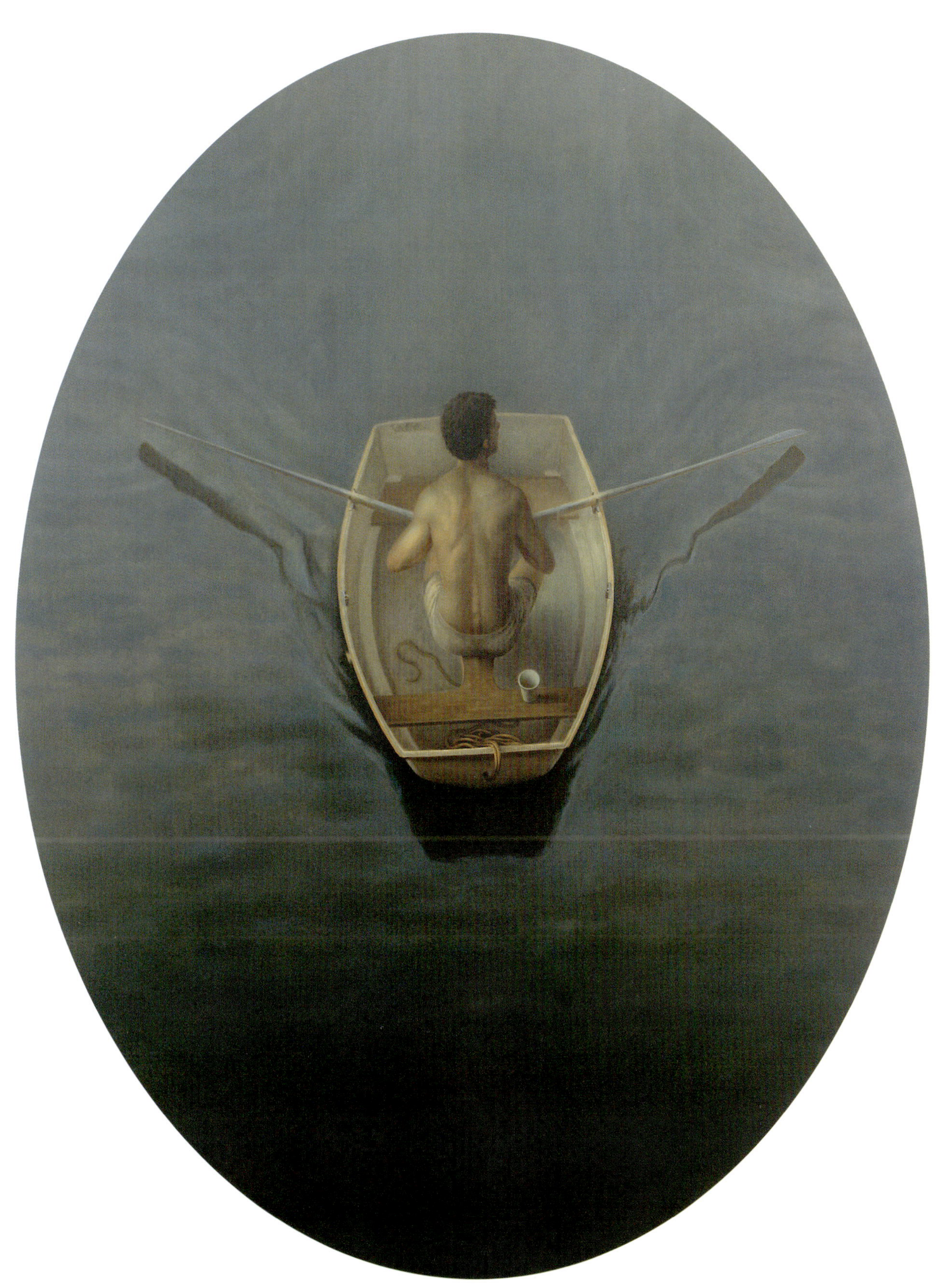

Pᴀssᴀɢᴇs (ʀᴇsᴏʟᴜᴛɪᴏɴs)

2001

Oil on linen on panel

37.5 x 35.5 ɪɴᴄʜᴇs

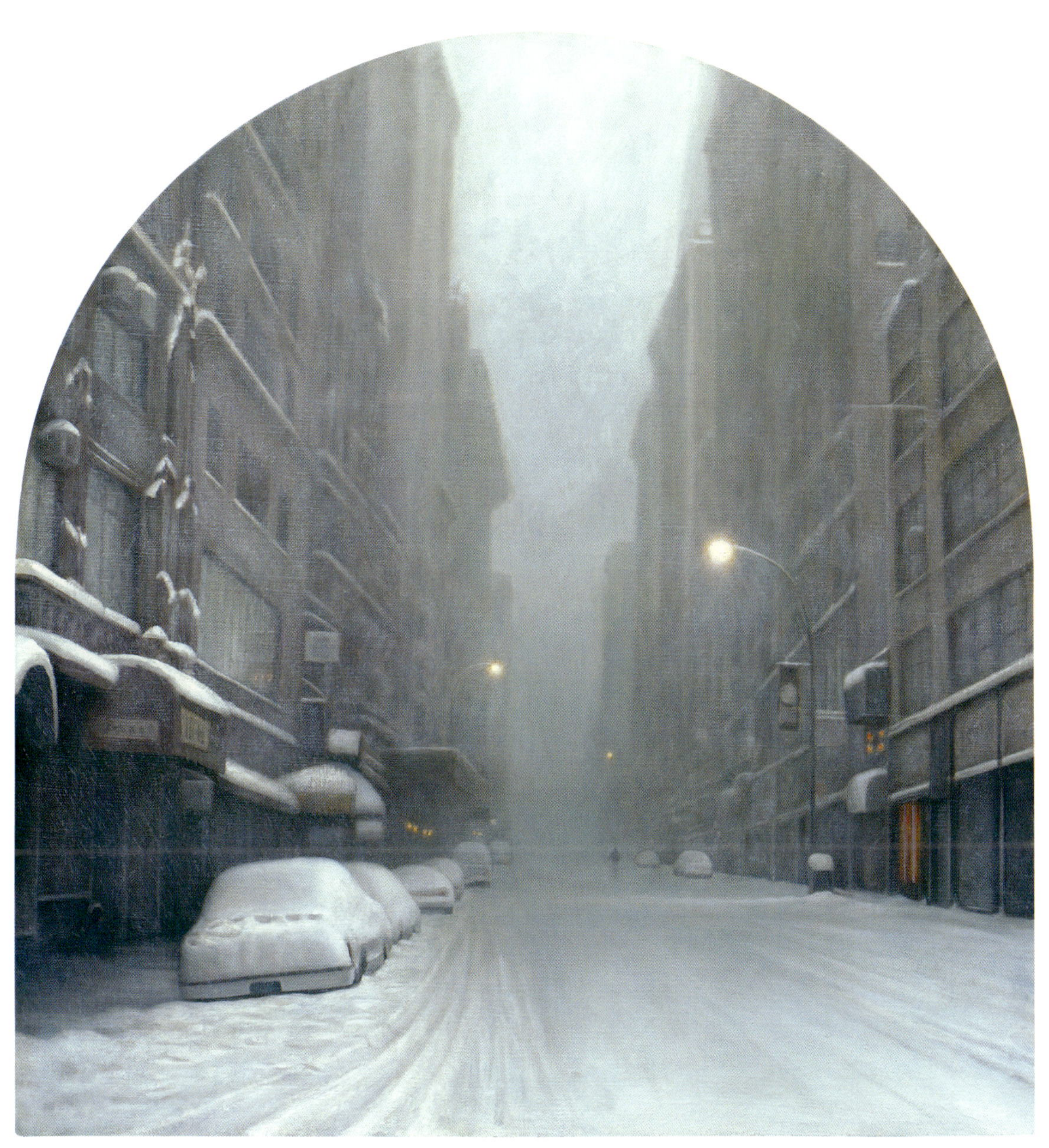

Visitors

2000–2001

Oil on linen on panel

21 x 28 inches

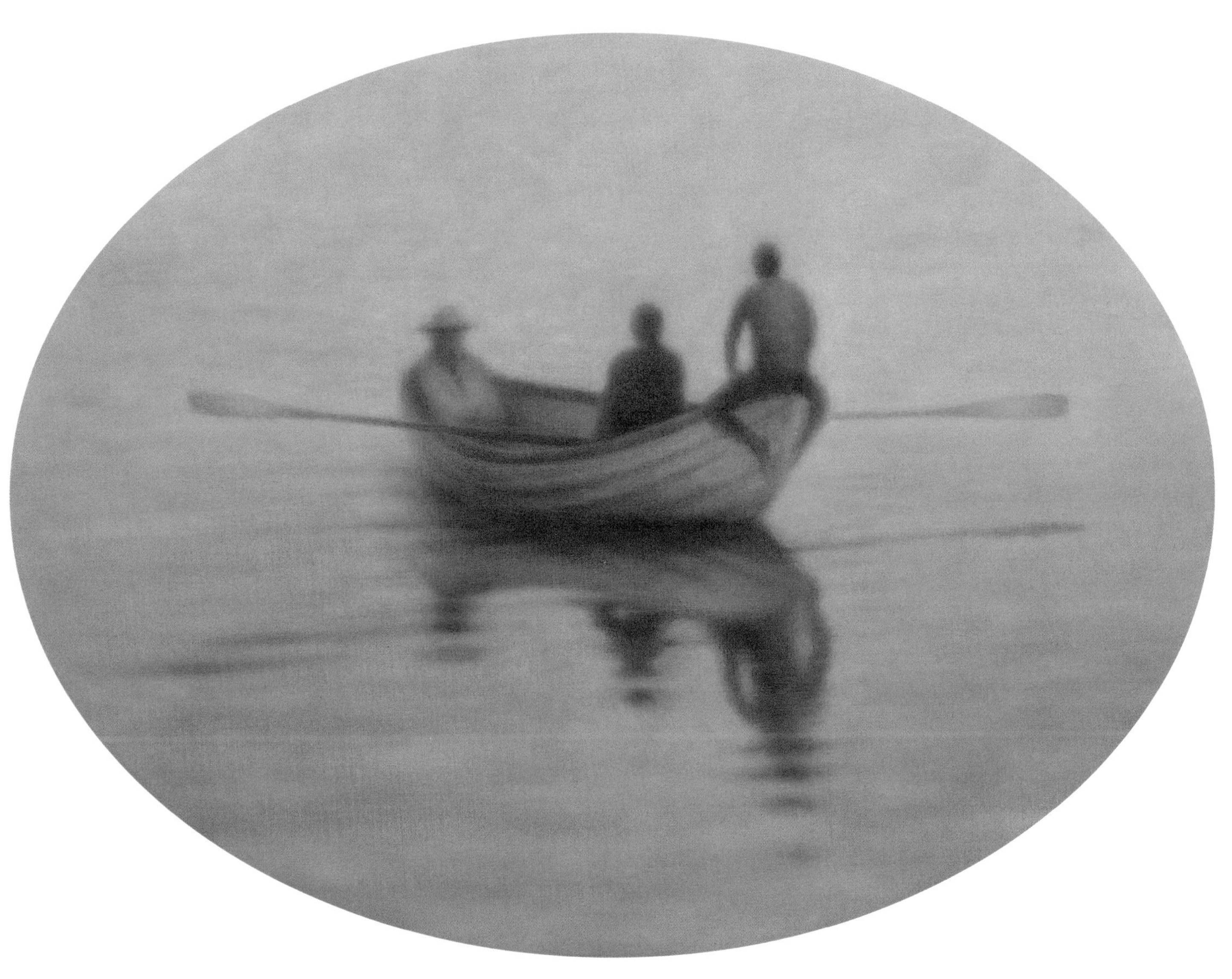

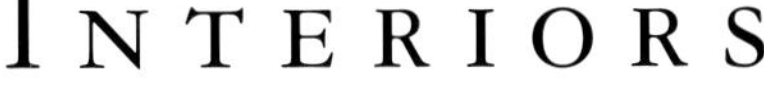

Interiors

Then and Now

1998

Oil on linen on panel

22 x 34 inches

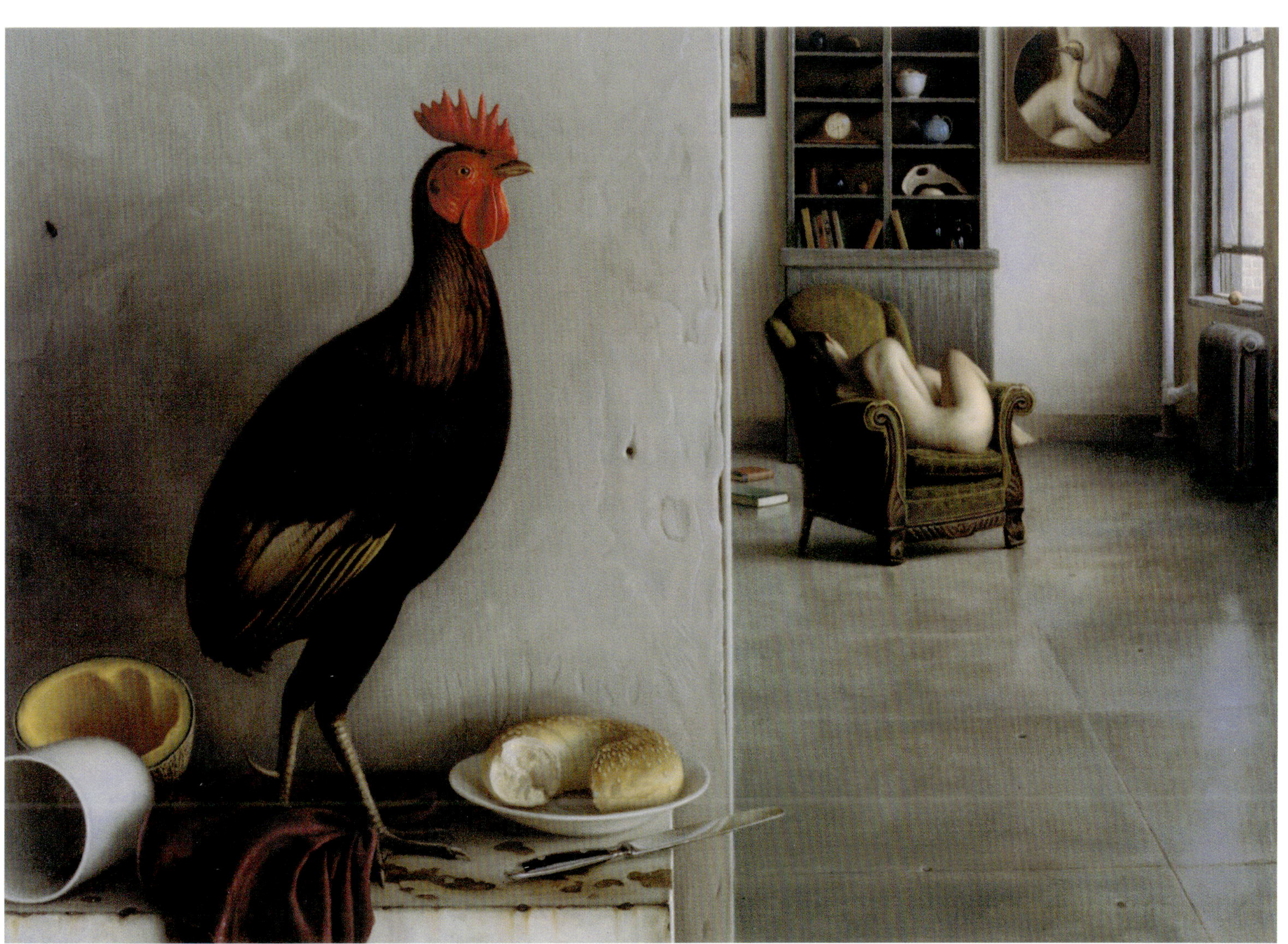

CONVERSATION

1996–1997

Oil on linen

65 X 40.5 INCHES

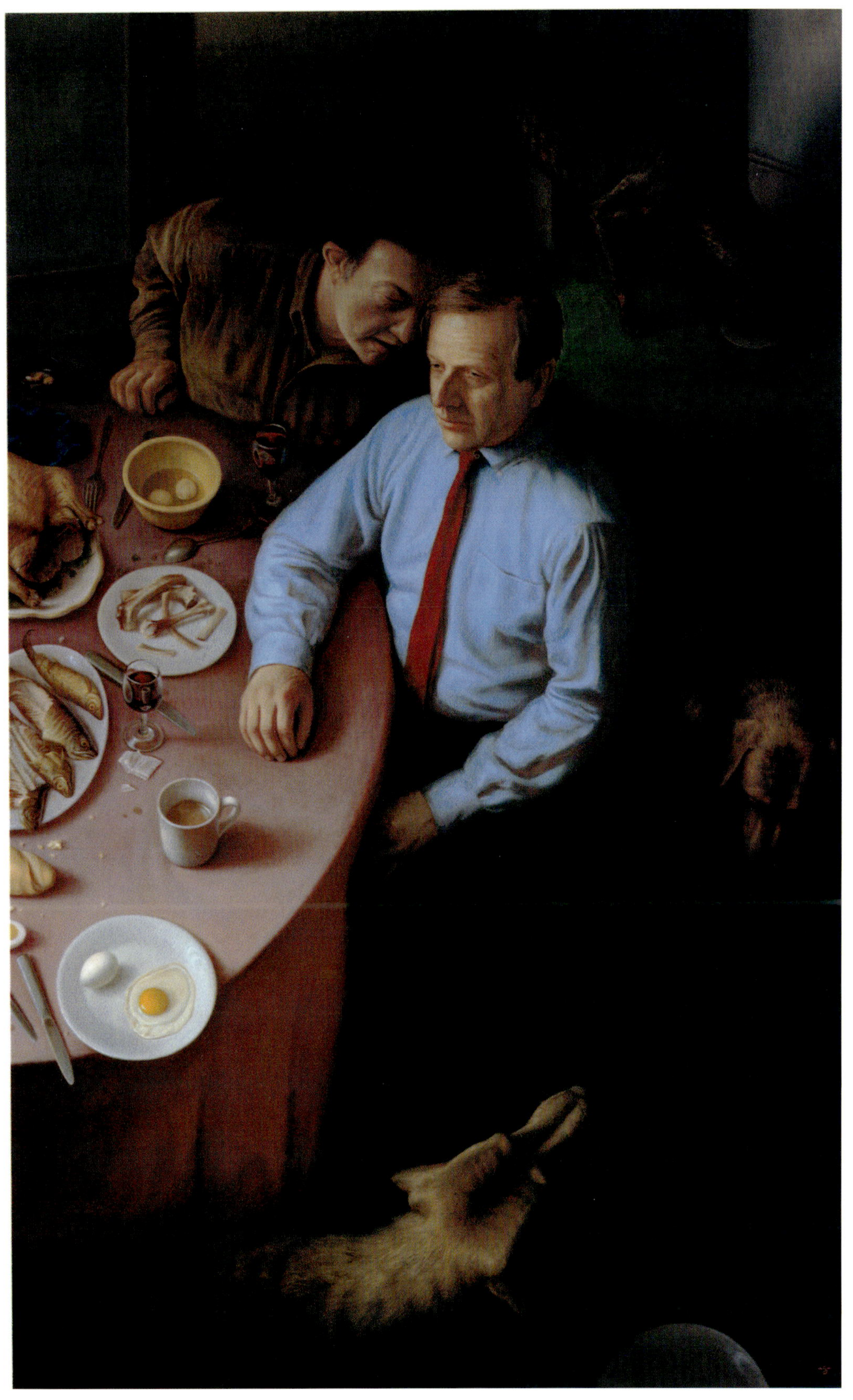

WOMAN WITH PIG

2000–2001

Oil on linen

48 INCHES

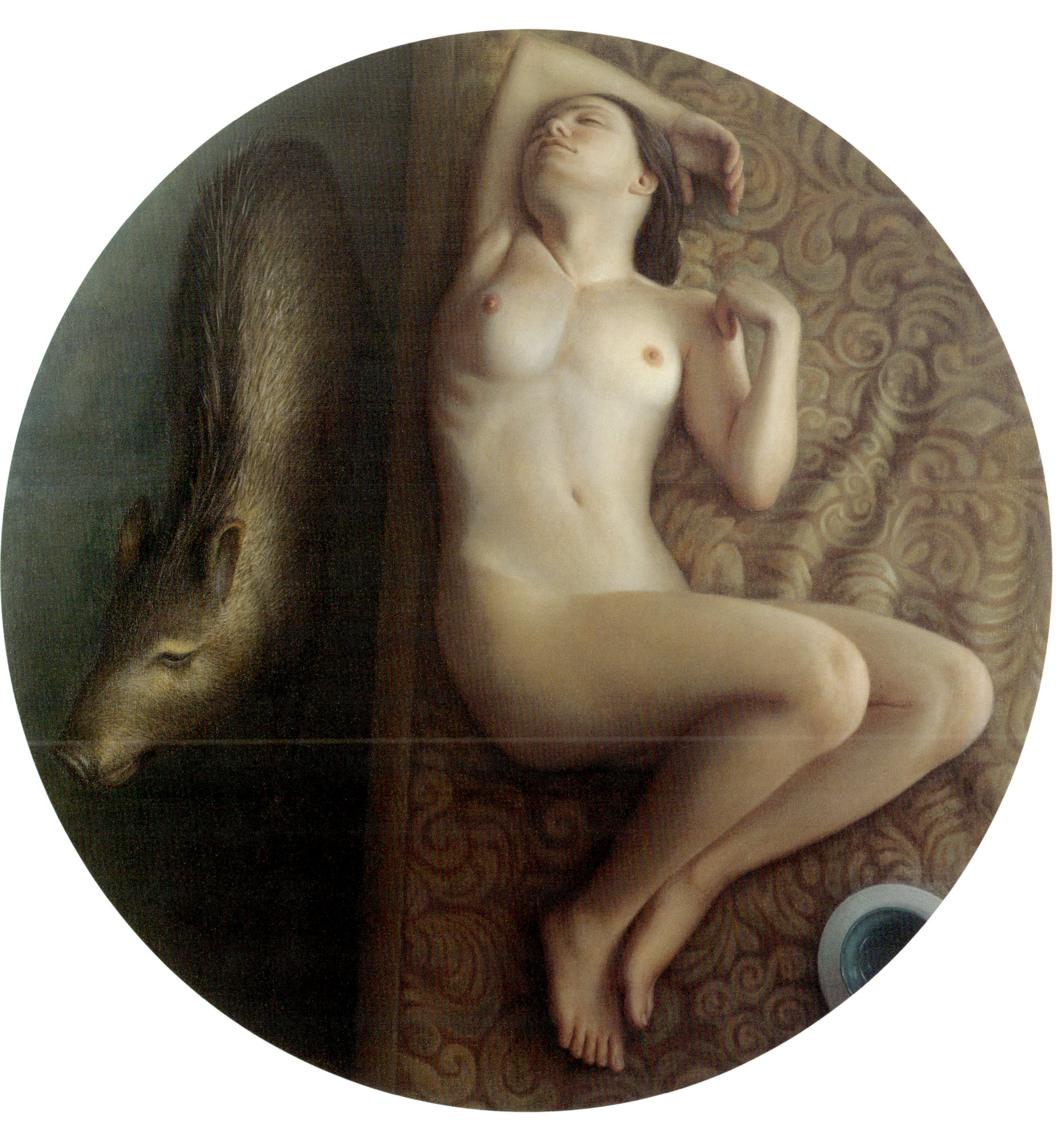

Man Entering Room

(Reoccurrence)

2000–2001

Oil on linen

72 inches

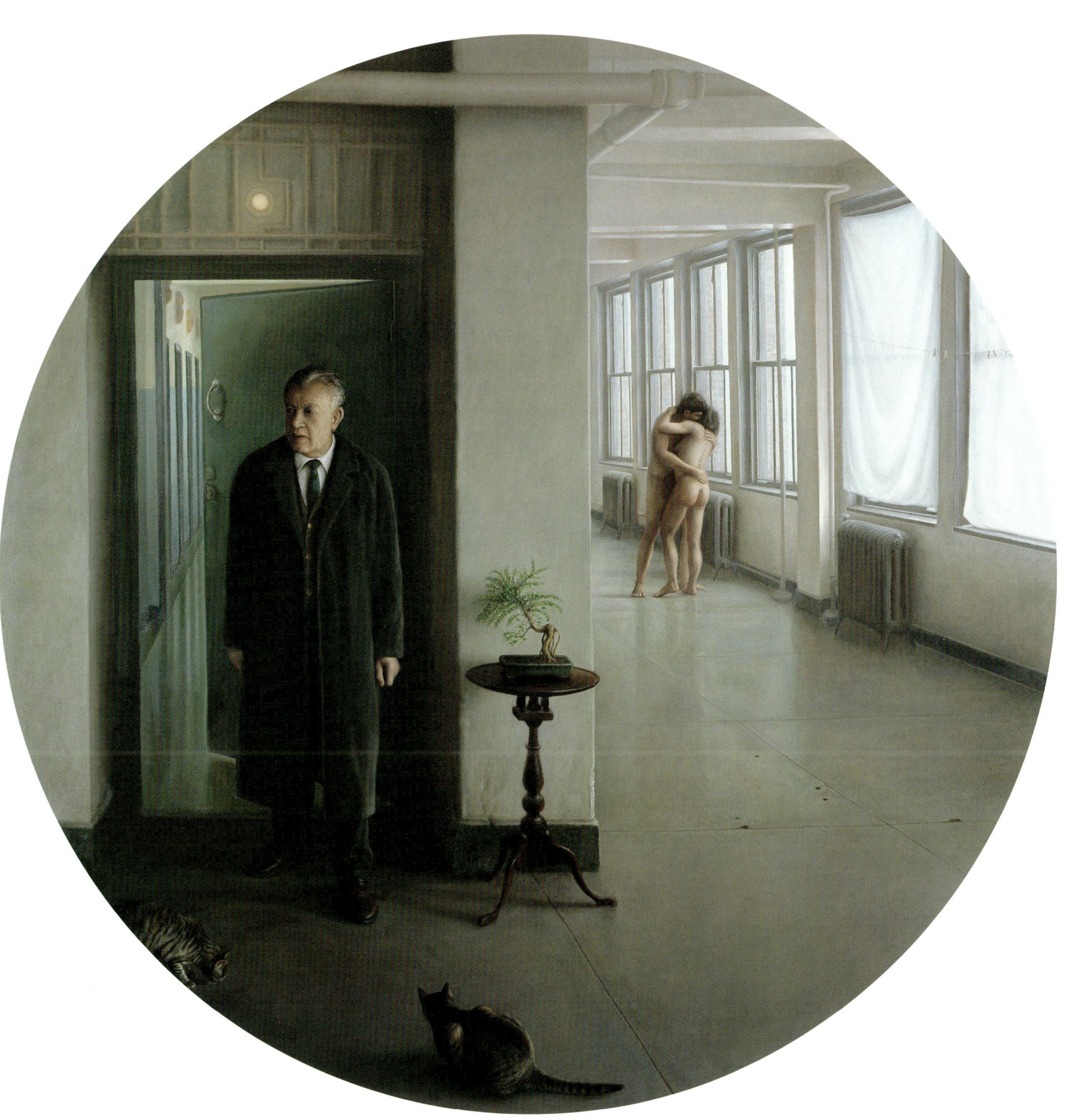

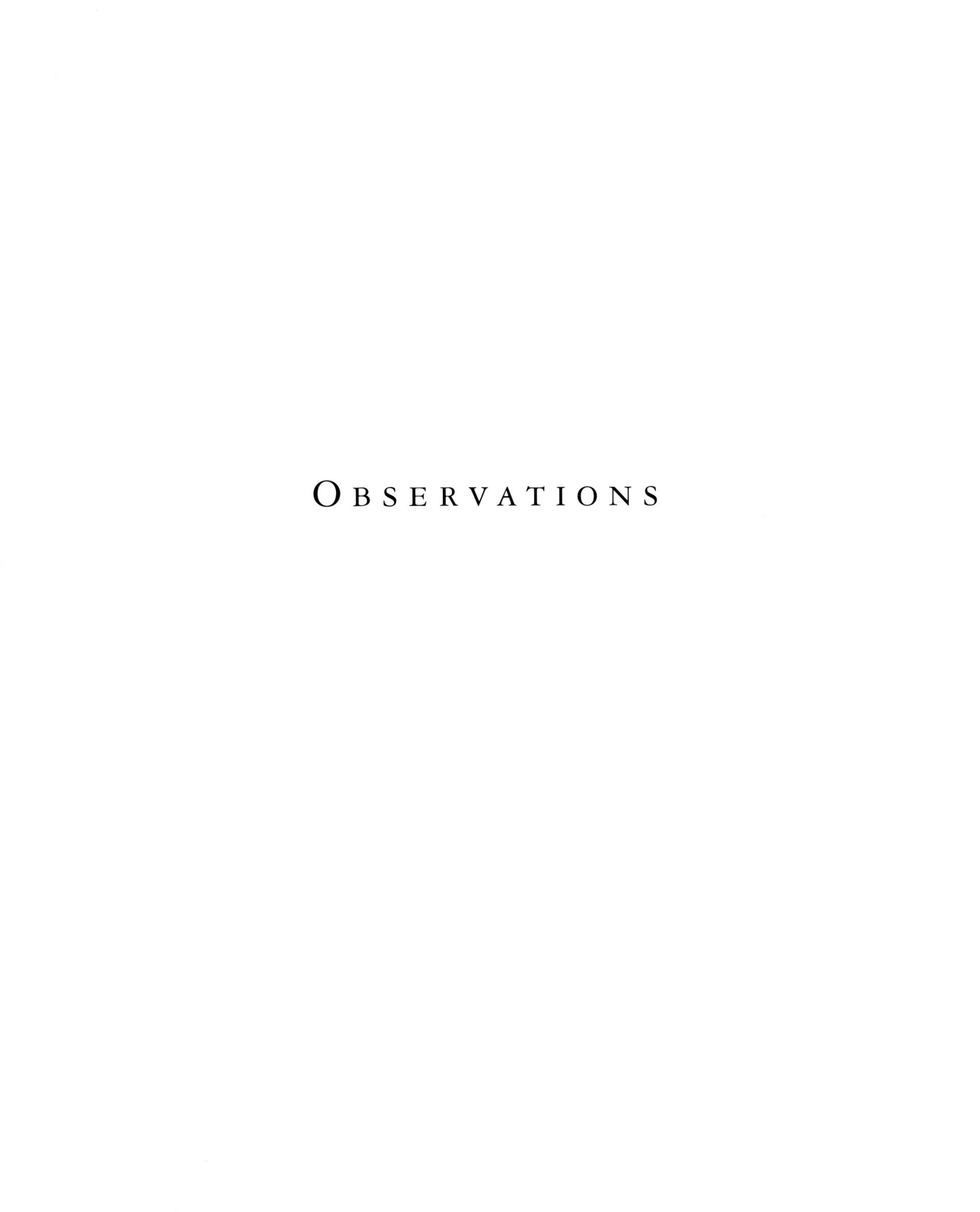
Observations

CRAB IN A PAN

1999

Oil on linen on panel

17 INCHES

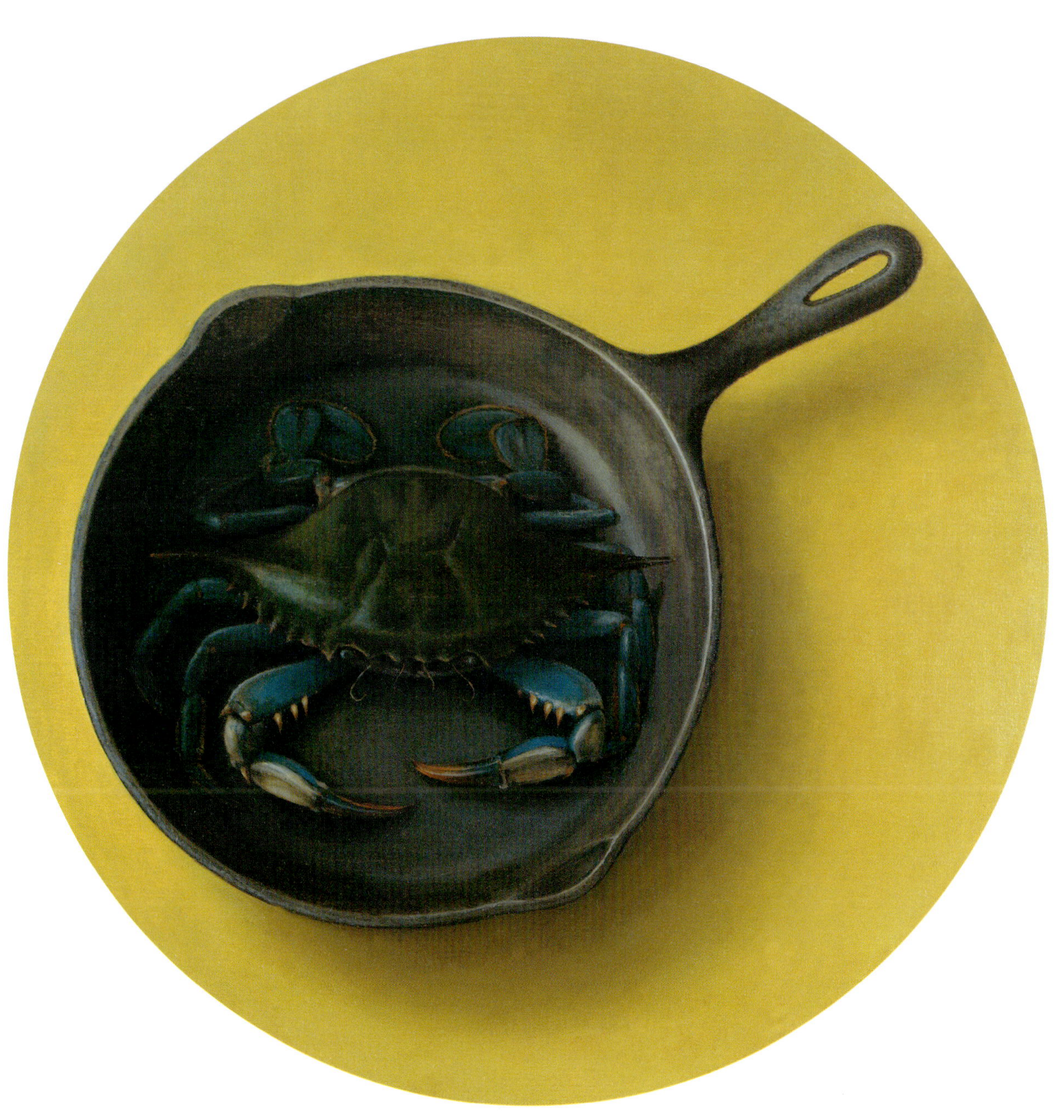

Fish and Bones

1997–1999

Oil on linen on panel

14.5 X 12 INCHES

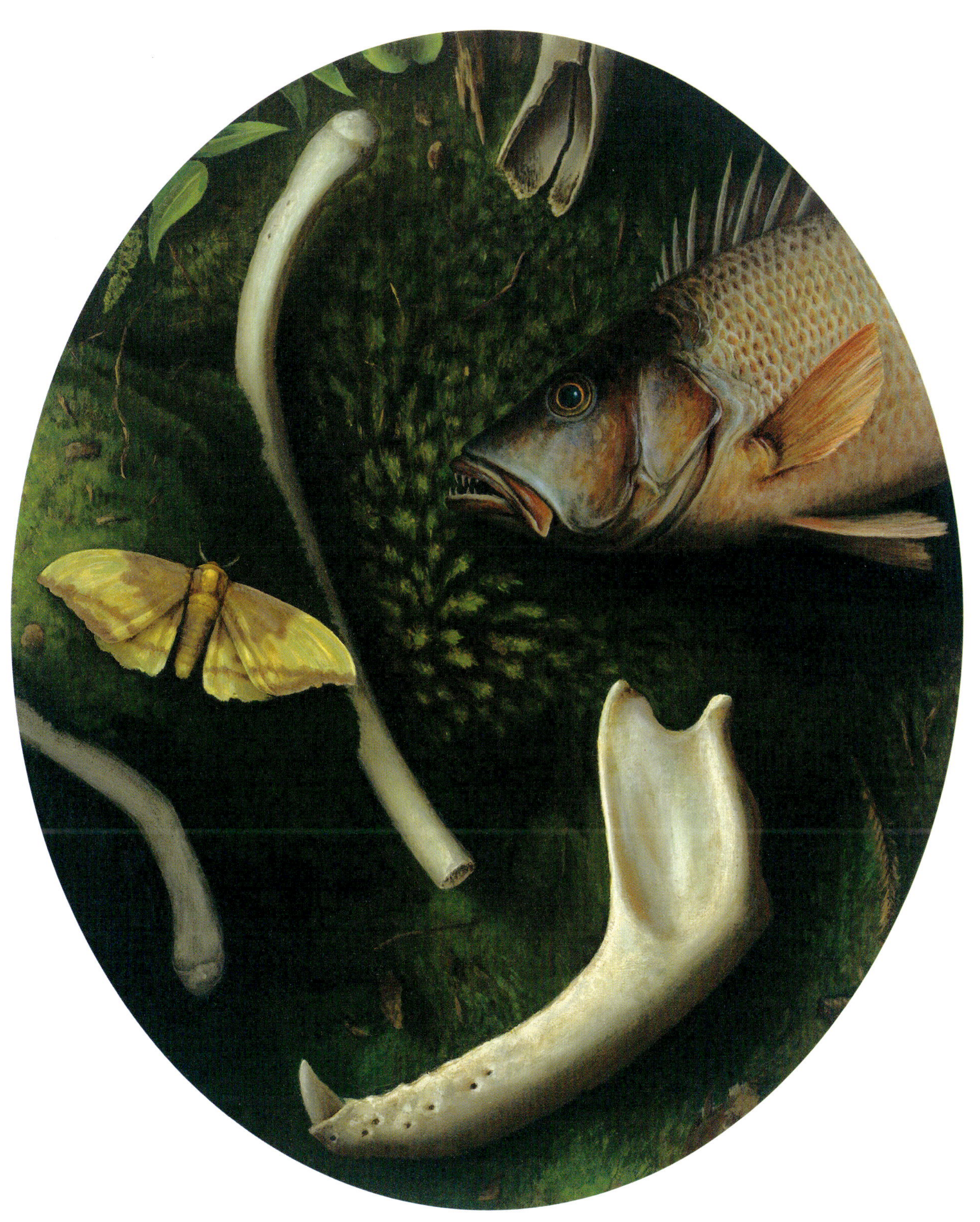

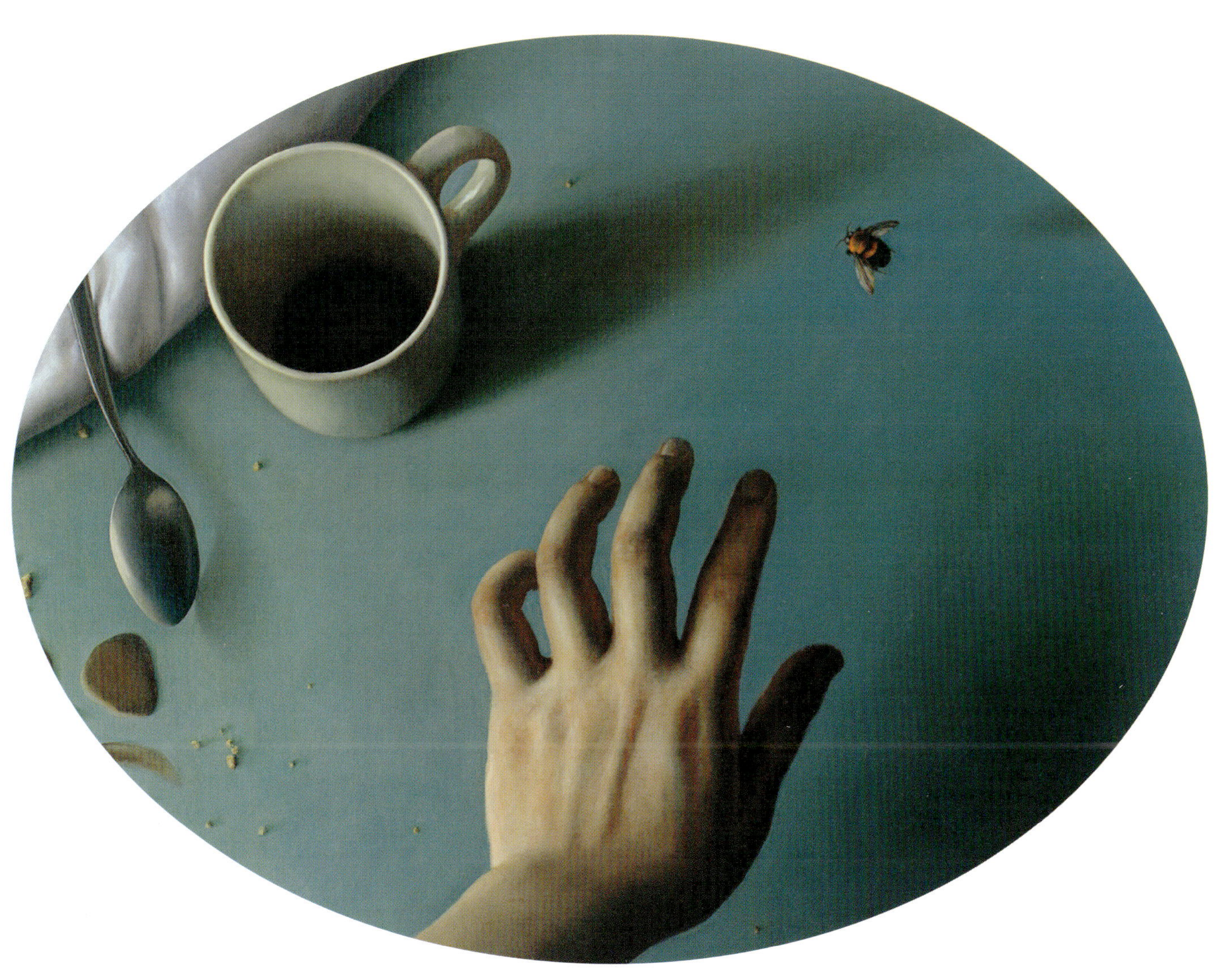

WADE SCHUMAN

Born: July 12, 1962, Cambridge, MA

EDUCATION

1983-86   Pennsylvania Academy of the Fine Arts, C.F.A.

1980-81   Rhode Island School of Design, Foundation Program

SELECTED EXHIBITIONS

2001-02   *Wade Schuman*, solo exhibition, Forum Gallery,
New York, NY

2000   *Art from The Sciences*, curated exhibition.
Locations: New York Academy of Sciences, New York, NY,
Binghamton University Art Museum, Binghamton, NY
The National Academy of Design 175th Annual Exhibition,
New York, NY
Contemporary Art from a Figurative Perspective, curated exhibition,
The Gallery of Contemporary Art, Sacred Heart University,
Fairfield, CT

1999-00   *Re-Presenting Representation IV*, curated exhibition,
Arnot Art Museum, Elmira NY

1999   *Wade Schuman, Selected Works*, solo exhibition,
Huntington Museum of Art, Huntington, WV
Ex-capillary, curated exhibition, Allen Sheppard Gallery,
New York, NY
Still Lives, curated exhibition,
The Contemporary Art Center of Virginia, Virginia Beach, VA

1998   *The Figure*, group exhibition, Marcia Wood Gallery, Atlanta, GA
The Figurative Impulse, curated exhibition,
Kendell Campus Art Gallery, Miami Dade College, Miami, FL
Art Chicago 1998, Forum Gallery, The Navy Pier, Chicago, IL
San Francisco International Art Expo, Fort Mason Center,
San Francisco, CA
Still Life, curated exhibition, Forum Gallery, New York City, NY

1997   *Art Chicago 1997*, Forum Gallery, The Navy Pier, Chicago IL
The Derrière Guard, curated exhibition, The Kitchen,
New York, NY
Art At The Armory, Forum Gallery, New York City, NY

1996   *Nature Morte: Contemporary Still Life*, curated exhibition,
Museum of American Art of the Pennsylvania Academy of the
Fine Arts, Philadelphia, PA
Selections: 1984-1995, group exhibition, Creative Artist's
Network
Woodmere Art Museum, Philadelphia, PA
The Art Show, Park Avenue Armory, New York, NY

1995   *Hot*, curated exhibition, K&E Gallery, New York, NY
New Looks, group exhibition, Forum Gallery, New York, NY
The Spiritual Dimension, curated exhibition,
Suzanne H. Arnold Gallery, Lebanon Valley College of PA

1994   *Wade Schuman*, solo exhibition, Forum Gallery, New York, NY
Wade Schuman, solo exhibition, The More Gallery,
Philadelphia, PA
Art Miami, Forum Gallery, Miami, FL
Peaceable Kingdom, curated exhibition, Babcock Gallery,
New York, NY
The Art Show, Forum Gallery, Park Avenue Armory,
New York, NY
Figure Drawings, group exhibition, The More Gallery,
Philadelphia, PA

1993   *Art Cologne 1993*, Forum Gallery, Cologne, Germany
FIAC 1993, Forum Gallery, Grand Palace, Paris, France

1992   *Figurative Eight*, Delaware Center for Contemporary Art,
Wilmington, DE
Line as Language, Southern Alleghenies Museum of Art,
Loretto, PA

1992-93   *Hard Choices/Just Rewards II*, exhibition of Pennsylvania Council
on the Arts Visual Arts Fellows. Locations:
Johnstown Art Museum, Southern Alleghenies Museum of Art,
Johnstown, PA
Blair Art Museum, Southern Alleghenies Museum of Art,
Hollidaysburg, PA
University Art Gallery, University of Pittsburgh, Pittsburgh, PA
Everhart Museum, Scranton, PA Bruce Gallery, Edinboro
University of Pennsylvania, Edinboro, PA
Westminster College, New Wilmington, PA
The University of the Arts, Philadelphia,PA

1991   *Ten Contemporary Philadelphia Painters*,
Westmoreland Museum of Art, Greensburg, PA
Juvenilia: The Art of Future Past, Levy Gallery,
Moore College of Art and Design, Philadelphia, PA

1989-91   Selected member exhibitions, Creative Artists Network Gallery,
Philadelphia, PA

1990   *Philadelphia Art Now*, curated exhibition,
Philadelphia Museum of Art, Philadelphia, PA
Group Exhibition, Allan Stone Gallery, New York, NY

1989   *Biennial '89*, curated exhibition, Delaware Art Museum,
Wilmington, DE

1988   *Fellowship Exhibition of the Pennsylvania Academy of the Fine Arts*,
Port of History Museum, Philadelphia, PA

1987   *Exhibition of Pennsylvania Artists*, The State Museum, Harrisburg, PA
The Philadelphia Eye, curated exhibition, Pace University Gallery, New York, NY
Group Show, Asuno Gallery, Washington, D.C.

1982-86   *Summer Exhibition of Prize-winning Work*, Pennsylvania Academy of the Fine Arts, Philadelphia, PA

1985   *Fellowship Exhibition of the Pennsylvania Academy of the Fine Arts*, Peale House Gallery, Philadelphia, PA

SELECTED AWARDS

1999   Walter Gropius Masters Workshop Lecture, Huntington Museum of Art, Huntington, WV

1996   Finalist for painting, NEA/MAAF Regional Fellowship, Painting Fellowship, Pennsylvania Council on the Arts

1995   Finalist for painting, Elizabeth Foundation for the Arts

1994   Painting Fellowship, Pennsylvania Council on the Arts

1991   Painting Fellowship, Pennsylvania Council on the Arts

1990   Award of Excellence, Philadelphia Museum of Art, Philadelphia, PA

1988   The Mary Post Prize for Painting, P.A.F.A Fellowship, Port of History Museum, Philadelphia, PA
York Springs Award, State Museum, Harrisburg, PA

1987   Commission for large painting, ARA Services Inc. Philadelphia, PA

1982-86   Awards and Honors, Pennsylvania Academy of the Fine Arts:
Scheidt Traveling Scholarship for study in Europe
Benjamin West Prize for Outstanding Technique
Cecilia Beaux Portrait Prize
Daniel Garber Prize for Drawing
Morris Blackburn Print Prize
Alexander Prize
Small Black and White Print Prize
Charles Toppan Prize

SELECTED BIBLIOGRAPHY

2001   Brooker, Niccoló, *Drawings by 20th Century and Contemporary Masters*, exhibition catalogue, Forum Gallery.

1999-00   O'Hern, John D., *Re-Presenting Representation IV*, exhibition catalogue, Arnot Museum of Art, ill. p.31.

1997   Brown, Gerard. *Same Planet, Different Worlds*, The Philadelphia Weekly.

1996   Sozanski, Edward. *Art*, The Philadelphia Inquirer.

1994   Sozanski, Edward. *Art*, The Philadelphia Inquirer.
Gallini, Mark. *The Beauty of the Beast*, Seven Arts Magazine.
Holsten, Glen. *Wade Schuman, The Seven Deadly Sins*, Television Spotlight, Artist Profile, WHYY, TV12.

1992   Banai, Paul. *Line as Language*, exhibition catalogue, Southern Alleghenies Museum of Art.

1991   *Contemporary Philadelphia Artists*, exhibition catalogue, Philadelphia Museum of Art Publications, ill p.119.
Hard Choices/Just Rewards, exhibition catalogue, Pennsylvania Council on the Arts, ill. p.19.
Frisk, John. *Ten Contemporary Philadelphia Painters*, exhibition catalogue, Westmoreland Museum of Art.

PUBLISHED

1998   *The Sciences Magazine*, New York Academy of Sciences, May-June, 1998, ill. pp.40-42.

1996   *The Beak of the Finch* by Jonathan Weiner, Recorded Books Inc., cover image.

1992   *Boulevard Journal of Contemporary Writing*: Vol. VII, Nos. 2&3, cover images.
Boulevard Journal of Contemporary Writing: Vol. VII, No. 1, ill. pp.22-25.

TEACHING AND OTHER

1989-02   Private Atelier, New York, Philadelphia, painting and drawing instructor.

1994-02   Graduate School of Figurative Art of the New York Academy of Art, New York, NY, faculty, painting, drawing, art history.

1992-98   The Pennsylvania Academy of the Fine Arts, Philadelphia, PA, faculty, painting and drawing.

1990-92   Academy of Natural Sciences, Philadelphia, PA, painting and drawing instructor.

2000-02   RBS Gazette, New York, NY, Acting Creative Director, Senior Editor.

1999-02   HAZMAT Modine, band founder, leader, writer, performer.

FORUM GALLERY

745 FIFTH AVENUE, NEW YORK, NEW YORK 10151

TELEPHONE 212-355-4545, FACSIMILE 212-355-4547

www.forumgallery.com

Cover, detail from: FISH AND BONES, 1997–1999

CATALOGUE DESIGNED BY WADE SCHUMAN AND IMPRESS, INC., NORTHAMPTON, MASSACHUSETTS   PRINTED IN CHINA

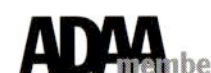